Feeding Your Soul with Food from the Father's Table

30 Daily Inspirational Devotions

by Dr. Willie R. Hill Sr.

DORRANCE PUBLISHING CO
EST. 1920
PITTSBURGH, PENNSYLVANIA 15238

Dorrance Publishing Co
585 Alpha Drive
Pittsburgh, PA 15238
Visit our website at *www.dorrancebookstore.com*

ISBN: 979-8-89027-027-6
eISBN: 979-8-89027-525-7

DISCLAIMER

Due to the significant amount of material and topics that I have used in my book I felt that it is necessary to post this disclaimer on all themes and subject matter that is in the book. These topics are inspired by the Holy Spirit and are original to the author. While ideas and illustrations are often gleaned from many other sources, the topics and subject matters are unique to the author and may be freely used to preach, teach, and richly bless the people of God in any way, as you read this book. My sincere desire is that all who read this book will be enriched and blessed in many ways: I hope that you will find favor and love with God and man. All scriptures come from the Holy Bible the King James Version and are used to help you to better understand the topics and what God's Word is saying to you. May the blessing of God rest upon you as you read this book. Amen.

FORWARD

Sometimes you can look at other people's lives and can be amazed at the things they have been able to accomplish in the time that they are here, especially when it appears that they always have so much stacked against them, well this is the case with the author. Born May 11th, 1956 to the late Elder Rufus Hill Sr and Pastor Lacie E. Hill in Flint, MI, Willie R. Hill was the second to last child of six children; twin girls and four boys. He experienced tragedy at the age of 10 when he lost his father, oldest and youngest brother in a car wreck that also left him and his other brother in full body cast for a year and his mother with a broken back as well as his sister with injuries to her head. It wasn't enough that he lost so much that day, but it happened on his tenth birthday. Yes, I know that this seems like too much personal information, but I guarantee that it speaks volumes to the character of this man. Through this very tragic event, he took on many roles to many people, often seeming to overload himself to make things easy for others. He has had the opportunity to accomplish many things that we have witnessed in our lives, from becoming a barber while working full time with a family, to earning several degrees including a Ph.D., just to name a few. The author's passion and zeal for God and His word is evident in his daily life and he has impacted so many lives through his words, his ministry and the example that he shows daily. I know that it can be thought of as biased because of our relationship to the author, but there is no one better that we know, then our father Pastor Dr Willie R. Hill Sr. Ph.D.

Willie Jr, Talecia and Krystal Hill

I WOULD LIKE TO DEDICATE THIS BOOK TO THE ONE PERSON WHO KNEW I AM A REAL CHRISTIAN IN EVERY SENSE OF THE WORD. THERE ARE SOME THAT PREACH AND TEACH ABOUT JESUS WHILE STANDING BEFORE OTHERS, BUT WHEN THEY ARE ALONE, THEY ACT OTHERWISE (AS A COUNTERFEITER, IMITATION, FRAUDULENTLY). THIS WOMAN LIVED HER LIFE AS IF CHRIST WAS COMING BACK THAT SAME DAY. SHE WAS ONE THAT ALWAYS TAUGHT ME TO DO WHAT IS RIGHT EVEN WHEN PEOPLE TREATED ME WRONG, ONE THAT ALSO TAUGHT ME HOW TO WALK IN A WAY THAT GOD CAN GET THE GLORY AND BE PLEASED WITH MY LIFE. ONE WHO BELIEVED IN FASTING AND PRAYING CONTINUALLY, SEEKING GOD FOR THE ANSWERS TO THEIR EVERY NEED. I WATCHED THIS PERSON ALL OF MY LIFE AND ALL THAT I COULD SEE WERE HER CONTINUOUS EFFORTS TRYING TO PLEASE GOD IN EVERY WAY AND IN EVERYTHING THAT SHE DID. SHE TAUGHT ME HOW TO WALK RIGHT BEFORE GOD, HOW TO TREAT MY FELLOW MAN THE WAY THAT I WANTED TO BE TREATED AND EVEN IF THEY TREATED ME WRONG TO LOVE THEM ANYHOW, THAT NO MATTER WHAT, GOD SEES IT ALL. SHE TAUGHT ME HOW TO PRAY, WHEN TO PRAY AND WHAT TO PRAY FOR. PRAYER PLUS FAITH WILL EQUAL YOUR ANSWER TO EVERY SITUATION THAT COMES IN YOUR LIFE. EVEN WHEN HER FAMILY WAS IN A TRAGIC ACCIDENT, KILLING HER HUSBAND AND TWO SONS. LEAVING HER AND TWO OF HER CHILDREN IN THE HOSPITAL WITH BROKEN AND FRACTURED BONES NOT KNOWING WHETHER SHE WOULD LIVE OR DIE, SHE ALWAYS KEEPS HER TRUST IN GOD AND HIS WORD. HER TWO SONS LAY IN THE HOSPITAL IN BODY CASTS AND SHE WAS NOT ABLE TO SEE THEM FOR WEEKS, BUT SHE STILL TRUSTED IN GOD IN EVERY WAY THAT SHE COULD. MISTREATED, TALKED

ABOUT, LIED ON, STOLEN FROM, SUED BY HER OWN FAMILY, YET SHE STILL SHOWED CHRISTIAN LOVE TO EVERYONE WHO MISTREATED AND ABUSED HER. A YOUNG WOMAN THAT HAD BEEN APPROACHED ON MANY OCCASIONS TO MARRY BUT BECAUSE SHE DID NOT WANT ANYONE TO HARM HER CHILDREN, SHE DENIED HERSELF OF MARRIAGE AND COMPANIONSHIP. SHE LIVED, PREACHED, AND TAUGHT HOPING THAT OTHERS WOULD COME TO CHRIST AND BELIEVE AS SHE BELIEVED. AT THE AGE OF 92, SHE SHOWED ME THE GREATEST LESSON OF ALL WHICH WAS HOW TO SUFFER FOR RIGHTEOUSNESS SAKE, SO TODAY THIS BOOK IS DEDICATED TO MY MOTHER THE LATE PASTOR LACIE E. HILL.

Table of Contents

DAY 1: What if you had a reset button for your life?

Have you thought about the past and how much better things would be if you could do it all over again? What a question to think about huh? We can't look into the future to see what life has in store for us, but if we could, no one would ever make any mistakes or poor decisions. Everyone would try to live their lives differently than what they do now. We would eliminate the possibility of encountering bad experiences, even those that have made us stronger, smarter, and/or wiser. Despite that, we cannot change our past. It will always be just that, and those choices or mistakes rather good or bad, we must live with. The good thing is that we can change our futures.

We can change what we are doing now and what we will do in the future. The decision is up to us. So many people carry many regrets from their past decisions which have stunted their abilities to move forward in their lives. They are incapable of having meaningful relationships with other people because they haven't forged ahead from the past. They are virtually stuck in the past and have not found closure from those situations. Ask yourself "if I could start all over again and just push the rewind button, would I?." Would you do things differently or would it be the same? As a counselor, I believe that some people, no matter how bad their situation, will always do things the same way. I have found that it is very difficult for some people to change. This could be accredited to a love for living on the edge, a need to be in control, or an inability to see potential threats in their environment.

For others it could be as simple as seeking the feeling of "freedom" from family and judgment. There's a popular saying that states "The past is the past," but this statement should include that we must move forward while letting the past be the past. No matter how good or bad it was, it was our past, and we can't go back and change anything. At this point, it is important to focus on the lesson in our experiences while not dwelling on the experience.

Here's a look into what the Bible tells us in Philippians 3:13b-14: "But this one thing I do, forgetting those things which are behind, and reaching forth unto those things which are before. I press towards the mark of the prize of the high calling of God in Christ Jesus." How many times have we regretted and felt sorry for ourselves? Were you disappointed in how your life turned out or even distressed about past events that you could not change? You begin to look for a way to overcome those regrets, but do not realize that there is no such thing as a life without some regrets and sorrows.

However, you don't have to let it be a burden that will interfere with your present and future. Regrets are like a pebble thrown in a clam body of water. All it takes is one pebble to send ripples in your life, but just like the river, the ripples will soon become calm again, this is how the circle of life goes. Sometimes we are the pebbles in our own lives. Not allowing ourselves to find peace because we won't let go of our past. So let us think about our actions, the things we say, and who we surround ourselves with. So that tomorrow we won't have any regrets about what we have said or done today.

DAY 2: Why must we analyze everything before we do it?

Sometimes it's best to take a moment to think before we speak, because once it's out there, it's out there and you cannot take it back. This can be done by analyzing the situation before providing a response. Analyzing a situation is to study or determine the nature and relationship of the material that you are dealing with, which many people don't take the time to do. Saying exactly what is on your mind is not always the best approach. Subconsciously, it may seem like it was the right thing to say at that moment, but historically, war and fighting have taken place because someone didn't take the time to think about what they were saying, and to whom they were saying it. Yes, there are some that will say whatever comes to their minds no matter what the consequences are, but this doesn't justify the negative consequences that come with their actions. Let's look at what the scripture has to say about this. "But the tongue can no man tame; it is an unruly evil, full of deadly poison." (James 3:8) This scripture outlines the fact that our tongue alone can be the source of discourse among people simply because it's hard to control. Now let's look at the opposing side. There are some people who over analyze every situation. They go as far as not speaking up for themselves even when it could cause them to be placed in a dangerous situation. Every situation that they deal with, they overthink it and try to come up with a rational decision. Sometimes resulting in them disassociating from the problem as a form of protection, being incapable of focusing on the things that are the most important in their lives or the things that surround them. They don't have a problem formulating thoughts in their mind, but they do have a problem saying what's on their mind and what they are thinking. The Bible tells us in the book of Proverbs 21:23: "Whosoever keepeth his mouth and his tongue keepeth his soul from troubles." This verse is telling us that we must be aware of what comes out of our mouths because there could be negative consequences. If we take time to analyze situations before determining a reaction, then we could reduce the chances of a misunderstanding. The Bible also says, "The power of life and death is in the power of the tongue." (Proverbs 18:21) This scripture highlights how much power our words truly hold. So, let us use the power that God has given us to make our lives and the lives of others better.

DAY 3: Am I a dependable person?

A question that we all should ask ourselves is can people trust me? More importantly, can God trust me? The only person that can answer that question is you. I often ask myself the questions; am I dependable, trustworthy, reliable, or responsible? Will I be there when someone needs me? Will I be on time? Will they have to ask me a second time? Will I let them down? Everybody is looking for that one person who is dependable. Are you that person? Would you consider yourself to be dependable and trustworthy?

Let's start with what it means to be trustworthy. A trustworthy person is someone in whom you can place your trust and confidence in and can rest assured that the trust will not be broken. To be trusted is a moral value and is considered a virtue. We as Christians should always try to have a trustworthy reputation where people can put their trust and faith in us as children of God. To be trusted is something that is earned over a period and does not happen overnight. Yes, trust is a fundamental moral and personal quality that God wants his people to have in their life since we are all in the image and likeness of God. Trust can rely on someone's good qualities. God and man want to have confidence in you but, do you have confidence in yourself? Isaiah 26:3-4: "Thou wilt keep him in perfect peace, whose mind is stayed on thee: because he trusted in thee. Trust ye in the Lord forever: for in the Lord Jehovah is the everlasting strength." How reliable are you? Can people rely on you?

When a person goes to the doctor, they go to him because they feel that he is suitable to meet their needs and to make them feel better. People go to their Pastor for counseling because they feel that they have faith in him to lead them in the right direction, and give them reliable information. As a Christian, we should hold ourselves accountable for every action that we do, and when we take responsibility for our actions, then we will be dependable in the eyesight of God and man.

DAY 4: ARE YOU AN SELFISH PERSON? DOES EVERYTHING HAVE TO BE ABOUT YOU?

Today's topic of selfishness is a concept that we all should reflect on often. Ask yourself, am I a selfish person? Do I have to always be the center of attention? When looking at a self- centered person, everything is always all about them. No matter what problem others may have, self-centered individuals are only concerned with themselves and what makes them happy and how your problems affect their lives. A self-centered individual is engrossed in oneself, one's affairs and not the needs of other people. Self-centered people do not like to be inconvenienced. So if someone is in need and asks for help, they may help if it doesn't interfere with what's going on in their lives. If it causes them to go out of their way, then the person who asks for help is out of luck. Self-centered individual problems are always worse than others. Self- centered people are usually stubborn, arrogant and egocentric. They always insist on having it their way, as opposed to following others who lead. The Bible said in the book of Roman 6:13: "Neither yields you your members as instruments of unrighteousness unto sin: but yield yourselves unto God, as those that are alive from the dead, and your members as an instrument of righteousness unto God." This kind of person loves to display their self-worth or self-importance often by an overwhelming, overpowering, dominating personality. In their own eyes, they are the most interesting person that they have ever met in their lives. Self-centered or selfish people refuse to submit (to yield to the power or authority of another) to anyone or anything but themselves.

They say that they love God, but that is as long as God is not the center of attraction. They don't want God to have more importance than themselves. God has tried to get these kinds of people to turn from their evil ways, but because of their self-centered and selfish nature, they refuse to, "As for the word that thou hast spoken unto us in the name of the Lord, we will not hearken unto thee. But we will certainly do whatever thing goeth forth out of our mouth." (Jeremiah 44:16- 17a) So ask yourself, am I self-centered? Am I dependable? Do I show compassion to my fellow man who is in need? Examine yourself if you find that you have a self-centered spirit. Ask God for forgiveness and pray for a loving, caring and giving spirit. It's never too late to change."I was a stranger, and ye took me not in: naked, and ye clothed me not: sick, and in prison, and ye visited me not." (Matthew 25: 43)

DAY 5: Do you find yourself easily offended or insulted?

Do you find yourself easily offended or insulted?

There are many ways that a person can be offended. The word offend is to cause displeasure, anger, resentment, and cause wounded feelings in a person. To offend God is to transgress His moral or divine laws: or just Sin. "But whoso shall offend one of these little ones which believe in me; it was better for him that a millstone was hanged about his neck, and that he were drowned in the depth of the sea. Woe unto the world because of offenses! For it must be; that offenses come; but woe to that man by whom the offense cometh." (Matthew 18: 6-7) No matter what you do or say, someone will always find a way to have an issue with you. They are so sensitive that you have to walk on eggshells not to offend them.

Sometimes people are just offended at the truth. John 8:32 says :" And ye shall know the truth and the truth shall make you free." This is simply because the truth will show them up and show exactly where they stand. They walk around angry and upset with you for something you are unaware of. In this state of mind they may think that you are talking about them or may have bad intentions toward them not fully understanding the meaning of what you said. They are on a constant emotional rollercoaster while allowing low self-esteem to drive them. Low self-esteem can negatively affect virtually every facet of your life, including your relationships, your job, and even your health. Low self-esteem is related to their psychological interpretation of the events that are going on around them.

No matter what you say, no matter what you do, some people will interpret what is said and done to them how they want to instead of how it was meant to be said or done. A lot of times some people have issues within themselves that have not been confronted. The Bible says in the book of Romans 14:13: "Let us not, therefore, judge one another anymore: but judge this rather, that no man put a stumbling block or an occasion to fall in his brother's way."

People are going to get offended at times, but do all you can do not to be the one to offend them, "God has called us to peace and not war."

DAY 6: GOD HAS A PLAN FOR YOU

So what are you waiting for, he included you too! Most people don't have a clue what the plan and the purpose is that God has for their life. They go through life clueless and never try to find out what God has in store for them. They just exist for a lifetime, wasting the time that God has given them to fulfill their purpose. God wants us (his people) to know what his plan and his purpose is in our lives. Psalm 32:8 reads: "I will instruct thee and teach thee in the way which thou shalt go: I will guide thee with mine eye." This scripture is confirming that God has a plan for you in every situation you face. We just have to seek him first to make sure that we align with his plan. How do we go about this? First of all we need to learn how to pray and what to pray for. By doing this simple first step it will set us on our way to an anchored prayer life. It is sad that so many people go through life, in the Church, wasting their God- given talent and time and never fulfilling the purpose nor plan that God had set forth before their birth.

Many go through their lives thinking what they are doing is all that they are supposed to do, but God has a higher purpose he intended for his people. In the book of Proverbs 23:7a Solomon said, "For as a man thinketh in his heart, so is he." To fulfill the plan of God. A person must believe that God has a plan for their life and know that they have to go to God in prayer to find out what that plan is. The enemy wants you to think that you are not good enough for God to use. He tries to defeat you before you can realize what God has put inside of you.

Even before your birth, he knows if you realize your potential then he will lose his power and control over you. He tries to keep you in a negative mind frame, so he can keep control over your life. The Bible says in the book of Jeremiah 1:5a: "Before I formed thee in the belly, I knew thee, and before thou camest forth out of the womb, I sanctified thee." So God let Jeremiah know before he came into this world that He had a plan and a purpose for his life, and God has a plan for everyone that will seek him to find out what that is. There are so many Christians walking around wishing that they could go forth as other Christians do, but still, they don't see the potential that they have in them. So you must not limit yourself to your own abilities but you must know through Christ all things are possible. At birth he created you with all the tools you would need to walk in his plan. You just have to believe, have faith, seek God, and continue in the plan and purpose that he has for you.

DAY 7: YOU WERE PICKED OUT, TO BE PICKED ON!

In the book of John 15:16a it states: "Ye have not chosen me, but I have chosen you, and ordained you, that ye should go and bring forth fruit, and that your fruit should remain."

"You were picked out, to be picked on."

The Bible states: "The world loves their own."

If you are a believer, the world cannot love you the way you think they should because: "You were picked out, to be picked on." When you go to work and people that you have been hanging out with for a long time begin treating you differently because of your new relationship with Jesus Christ. "You were picked out, to be picked on."

The Bible tells us that, "God will put no more on us then we can bear." When your family sees you coming and doesn't seem to be happy to see you but are happy to see you go, "You were picked out to be picked on." When you go to Church and the people in the Church, don't want you to be in their clique anymore, "You were picked out to be picked on." When you make a mistake and fall, and the people that should help you up are the same ones that are trying to keep you down, "You were picked out to be picked on." When it seems like you have more bad days then good days, or less money than more money, and all that you once had seems to be gone, "You were picked out to be picked on." When people you love lie to you, and it seems that everything is falling on you and you don't have anywhere to turn, "You were picked out to be picked on." Job was a man in the Bible that was picked out by God to be picked on by Satan. Job lived in the land called Ur, he was a man that was considered to be perfect and upright, and one that feared God, and eschewed evil and did everything that was good in the sight of God. He had seven sons and three daughters; he had great wealth, and he was called the greatest of all the men of the east. His family was a very close family.

"Now there was a day when the sons of God came before the Lord, and Satan came too. The Lord said to Satan why did you come here? Satan answered the Lord and said, from going to and fro in the earth, and walking up and down in it seeking whom I may devour. And the Lord said to Satan, have you considered my servant Job, there is none like him in all the earth. Then Satan answered the Lord, I have considered Job, but you won't let me touch him; take the hedge from around him and let me touch all that he has, and Job will curse you. So God let Satan touch all that Job had, but he could not touch Job's body."

When your enemies get you down, they try to keep you there until he can finish you off. Here Job is, he lost all of his children, all his wealth, all of his servants, and the Bible said, "All that he had was gone," but Satan was not finished with him yet. "Satan came before God again; he wanted permission to touch Job's body to show God that Job was serving Him only because God had protected him and made him wealthy. That if he could only touch Job's body, Job would curse God to His face. So God permitted him to touch Job's body, but Satan could not take Job's life. Job himself was stricken with a terrible skin disease, and he did not curse God nor did he blame God for his condition, but said: 'The Lord giveth, and the Lord taketh away blessed be the name of the Lord.'"

Job was picked out, to pick on. Like so many of believer's today, things come up in their lives that they don't understand. Many ask why it is so hard to find good jobs and good relationships. They wonder why their health is failing them and the answer is that you have been picked out to pick on. Like Job, he lost everything to show: "God's ways are not our ways and that his understanding goes beyond human understanding." We just have to have faith that when we are picked out to pick on, we can hold out like Job.

DAY 8: WE HAVE TO BUILD ACCORDING TO GOD'S PATTERN

So many people,when it comes to serving God, want to do things the way that they think it should be done and not the way in which the pattern has been set out. To build, you must first have to have a blueprint. That blueprint is the word of God; we cannot build on anything else. The Bible talks about building a house on sand, it will not stand, but if you build a house on "the rock" and that rock is Jesus Christ, it will stand forever. The way you live your life is the pattern that many people will see, and if we are professing Christ Jesus as our Lord and Savior, people should be able to see the pattern that the Bible talks about in our everyday living. The Bible says in I Timothy 1:16: "Howbeit for this cause I obtained mercy, that in me first Jesus Christ might shew forth all longsuffering, for a pattern to them which should here-after believe on him to life everlasting."

The Bible also says in Titus 2:7-8a: "In all things showing thyself a pattern of good works: in doctrine showing uncorruptness, gravity, and sincerity. Sound speech that cannot be condemned." People are always looking for some reason or excuse to change the way that God has set his patterns for their lives. It's easy to try to force into the pattern of others to fit in with the hype of their lives. while some might live in moderation, they will live in exaggeration causing them to live out of the will of God for their lives. As a Christian, do you realize that you might be the only bible that most people will ever read or even see in their lifetime?

If your foundation is not built on the right things, it's easy for you to feel that this is the plan that God has for your life. This way of thinking can cause and has caused numerous people to go astray due to their own personal beliefs that are not built on the foundation of Christ. Do you want to be the one that causes someone to stumble and fall because of the pattern that they see in your lifestyle? Do you want God to hold you responsible for the pattern that they are building? In order to build a solid foundation here are some examples of daily practices that can assist in developing and maintaining a solid foundation built on the principles of Christ. These include reading your bible daily, learning to love unconditionally, pray without wavering, and in every situation ask yourself what would Jesus do? These are a few tools that can be used to help you build and maintain your foundation in Christ in order to stand against the trials and tribulations that life has in store for us.

DAY 9: IT'S MORE THAN JUST A NAME!

Some people think that as long as they have the name of their religion or Church that they are going to heaven, and they act as if they don't have to live the life that God requires a true believer to live. It's more than just a name. They come to church on Sunday performing the same rituals all because of the name on the Church door. They feel that everything is alright with them and the Lord; because of the name that is on the church door. As a young boy, I could hear my mother say to me, "Son, it's a life that we must live unto God and a service that we must render unto him if we are going to be called a Christian." It's more than just a name. Because of a name, people mistreat each other. Because of the name, we have wars and fighting all over the world. Because of a name we have families separating themselves from each other. Because of a name, we have people that are living any and every kind of way but still saying they are going to heaven anyhow. It's more than just a name! Because of a name, men are fighting and killing their brothers. Mothers against their daughters, fathers against their sons. God's word says it would be this way in the end because people think and believe that it's all in the name. What matters most is the name that you call yourself and the relationship that you have with God the Father and his son Jesus Christ. Our focus must be on the relationship that we have with God, and not the name that is on the building. When we can get past holding more value in a title and focus more on the barriers being broken down in the lives of the believer and non believers then we can truly make progress.

Paul wrote in Ephesians about the unity of the believers in Ephesians 2: 19-20: "Now, therefore, ye are no more strangers and foreigners, but fellow citizens with the saints and of the household of God. And are built upon the foundation of the apostles and prophets: Jesus Christ himself being the chief cornerstone." People create religious beliefs because of a name; they also think and believe that they are the only one that can see it right. They only see what they want to see but for them to have a relationship with the Lord they must first have a relationship with people down here on earth.

We read in the book of Hebrews 2: 9-10: "But we see Jesus, who was made a little lower than the angels for the suffering of death, crowned with glory and honor; that he by the grace of God should taste death for every man. For it became him, for who are all things, and by whom are all things, in bringing many sons unto glory, to make the captain of their salvation perfect through sufferings." So now we can see and know that it's more than just a name, but it's about a relationship with Jesus Christ his Father.

DAY 10: ARE YOU KEEPING YOUR CHARGE?

When someone has a charge, they have a debt to be paid. Jesus paid our debt for our salvation; on the cross of Calvary, and gave up his life for our eternal salvation, so we can live eternally with God. As believers, we all have a charge (a duty, responsibility, and obligation) to keep a charge to walk right, a charge to live right, a charge to love all of God's people and a charge to obey God's word. Jesus also gave us a charge to go into the entire world and to make disciples of all men. He gives a direct charge to the believer in the book of Matthew 9:37-38: "Then saith he unto his disciples, the harvest truly is plenteous, but the laborers are few; pray ye, therefore, the Lord of the harvest, that he will send forth laborers into his harvest." This scripture gives us a view of what we see today with a church on every corner but a lack of people to fill them. There are still so many laborers needed but few to be found. There is much work to be done but few that are willing to accept their charge.

The bible says that "God gave his only son and his son gave his life so that we the true believer would have the right to life eternally." We all have work to do for the Lord and a date that we must pay. Sometimes we have to be reminded of our charge to keep faith with a pure heart, and of a good conscience.

I Timothy 1:14-15: "And the grace of our Lord was exceeding abundant with faith and love which is in Christ Jesus. This verse is a faithful saying, and worthy of all acceptation that Jesus Christ came into the world to save sinners." So if he is our Lord and gave us the charge, then we are to go out into the highway and hedges and invite God's people to come in.

Every day the enemy will try to stop you from keeping your charge, but it's up to you to hold on to God's unchanging hand because God has given you the power over the enemy and you can use your God- given power to keep your charge. I Timothy 1:18 Paul charges Timothy to keep his commitment to the LordL "This charge I commit unto thee, son Timothy, according to the prophecies which went before on thee, that thou by them mightest war a good warfare." You might have to fight to keep your charge that God has given you. What is most important is that we keep our heads up and our eyes toward the prize and keep moving forward to Christ and as long as you stay focused and committed to him then you will be able to keep your charge.

DAY 11: DO YOU KNOW HOW TO STTAY ON THE WALL?

The term staying on the wall means to be read to deafen or put up a barrier agent against the enemy when they come against the people of God. The wall that the bible is talking about is a structure that defines an area that surrounds the people of God. Staying on the wall is the call for a watchman to sound an alarm and that alarm was the blowing of the trumpet when he sees the enemy coming. There are three times recorded in the Bible when the trumpet was sound, the first one, in time of war, the second in a time of worship, and the third in a time of weddings. The watchman's job was to stand on the wall or in a watchtower and watch for the enemy invasion. The enemy comes in so many different ways trying to defeat the true believer in any way he can. He uses every trick in the book trying to tempt us so that we will come down from the wall. I Corinthians 10: 13: "There hath no temptation taken you but such as is common to man: but God is faithful, who will not suffer you to be tempted above that ye are able; but will with the temptation also make a way to escape, that ye may be able to bear it." That's why it is important to put up a barrier against the enemy. He will try to come into your heart and mind in so many different ways, that is why God has placed every Christian, every evangelist, every father, mother, pastor, and preacher on the wall because they are needed to stand. So when they see the enemy coming, they can sound the trumpet loud. Satan will try to attack your mind and preoccupy you with other things and people. This is done to cloud your mind and confuse you into falling into his traps. The Bible reminds us that we should always stay focused on Christ Jesus and not on the things of this world; because the enemy knows that if he can tempt your heart and mind then you will follow him.

Isaiah 26:3-4 states: "Thou wilt keep him in perfect peace, whose mind is stayed on thee: because he trusteth in thee. Trust in the Lord for ever: for in the Lord JEHOVAH is everlasting strength." The enemy will bring an assortment of problems, situations, troubles and misunderstandings into your life that could lead to depression, loneliness, sickness, doubts, anger, and fears. Which could be a result of your focus being taken off of the assignment that was given to you by God. The enemy will try to get you off the wall any way he can; it's your job to stay steady.

Philippians 4:7-9: "And the peace of God, which passeth all understanding, shall keep your hearts and minds through Christ Jesus. Finally, brethren, whatsoever things are true, whatsoever things are honest, whatsoever things are just, whatsoever are pure, whatsoever things are lovely, whatsoever things are of good report; if there be any virtue, and if there be any praise, think on these things. Those things, which ye have both learned, and received, and heard, and seen in me, do: and the God of peace shall be with you." We must remember to stay on the wall and stay focused while keeping our minds fixed on the things that God has set before us at all times. The enemy cannot steal the freedom that God has given to his people if we stay focused and always trust in God.

DAY 12: HOW AND WHY WE SHOULD BE MADE OVER

To be made over is to ask the Lord Jesus to come into your life and to forgive you for your sins. My mother always reminded me that life on earth is the place where the children of God get ready to live for eternity. Life of earth is temporary, it's a place to redress our lives or in other words to be made over in the image of our Lord and savior Christ Jesus. The title asked how and why we should be made over. The "how" is that one must realize that there is a need in their life for a change. Most people don't know or want to see that they need to make changes in their lives. They are in love with the world, the things of this world and not with the idea of eternal life with Christ Jesus. The "why" is, if we are not preparing to live with Christ for eternity, then we are getting ourselves ready to live in eternal damnation. Being made over is to make preparations for eternity with Christ Jesus. Some people believe that there is no life after death and living is all there is, but I beg to differ. If living was all there is to life, and there is no life after death then there would be no reason to live a Christian life, nor to go to church, nor to pray every day, nor to read the bible. There would be no reason to have the idea that we need to be made over. We the believers are the ones who know the truth; we know that there is life after death, and one day we will be with our Lord and savior Jesus Christ. John 17:2-3 says: "As thou hast given him power over all flesh, that he should give eternal life to as many as thou hast given him. And this is life eternal, that they might know thee the only true God, and Jesus Christ, whom thou hast sent."

God has a reason for your life on earth, and it doesn't stop here. God's purpose goes far and beyond more than just a lifetime. His plan for your life was established long before you were born. Do you know that God through his son Jesus Christ gave us the opportunity or the favor to be made over and to have a second chance for eternal life with him? If you have a personal relationship with Christ Jesus, you can say that you've been made over again, and the door to eternal life is open to you.

DAY 13: IT ONLY TAKES ONE TO MESS IT ALL UP!

My mother always said, "One bad apple spoils the whole bunch." Have you ever had a bushel of apples and one was bad, and you left it in with the other apples, and shortly the whole bushel had gone bad? If it only takes one apple that is bad, you know it only takes one person to mess it all up for many people. Think about it like this, when you're on the job and everything is going fine, and one person gets upset with the boss, everybody has to pay for what that one person has done. When you go to school, and one kid does something wrong, and because that kid did wrong all the other kids have to suffer the consequences because of it. The rules change, activities are taken away, and sometimes everyone has detention because of what that one kid has done. As a little boy, me and two of my brothers would always get in trouble with our mother for doing something wrong. When she would question us, the other two would not tell the one that did the wrongdoing, so our mother would punish all three of us for not tattling on the one that did wrong. In the story of Adam in the Garden of Eden; God commanded Adam to eat of every tree in the garden, but not of the tree of knowledge of good and evil. Because Adam disobeyed God by eating of the fruit, all mankind was punished for Adam's transgression which is evident even today. With all being punished just because of one man's wrongdoing. This story let us know that it only takes one to mess it all up for the rest. Adam messed it up for all mankind, but God had a plan to restore man back to his first estate.

Jesus Christ came to restore the way that God made it, and thanks be to God; Jesus fixed us back up and made it possible to once again fellowship with God the Father. By dying on the cross that is called Calvary, he restored the broken fellowship that man had once with God before Adam disobeyed and sin against God. So it took one to mess it up, and it took one to fix it back up. Don't be the bad apple that spoils the whole bunch.

DAY 14: ARE YOU SURVIVING THE TEST?

Every believer goes through a test. It does not matter how long you have been a Christian, nor the number of years you have been in the Church. Rest assured that at some point you will be tested, sooner or later. Most of the time another trial will come before you can manage to get over the test that you're battling. But there is a blessing coming your way if you just wait for it. Do you know that the way you handle the test and not allowing these trials to overcome you determines how God blesses you? It is always the enemy's job to make us fail our tests, causing us to repeat them; which hinders us from surviving every one of the obstacles that we go through. The Bible teaches us that: "the devil comes to still, kill, and to destroy, but God comes to give us life and that more abundantly." Sometimes the believer has to go through the refining process of life. The refining process is symbolic of the way that God purifies his people. The refining process means going through the fire of life so that when you come out, you will have changed from the old man to the new man who's created in the image of Christ Jesus.

It seems like things get hot and heavy, and hard to handle at times but God said, "It would not be easy, and he would not put; no more on you then you can bear." Sometimes you have to go through some things just to know where you are in Christ Jesus. Many people that have never had to go through anything feel that they are closer to God than the people that are going through problems and heartache in their everyday life, but the fact of the matter is if he never tests you, how then would you know where you are in him?

He already knows. After the test is over, then you too should know where you stand with the Lord. And yes, those people that never go through anything need to check their relationship with Christ because he told us in his word that we will have troubles in our Christian walk. I would like to ask you this question: how many times have you thought you were strong enough to go through situations just to find that your strength or your faith was weak? Just know that through the power of Jesus, you can defeat the enemy. "I can do all things through Christ who strengthens me."

All God wants us to do is to hold on and go through our test and trial, and he will refine you like gold out of the fire. Zechariah, 13:9: "And I will bring the third part through the fire, and will refine as gold is tried: they hear them: I will say, it is my people: and they shall say, the Lord is my God."

Have you been through the storms of life? Life brings some pretty bad storms, bad relationships, money problems, family problems, loss of jobs, loved ones passing, sickness in your body, and so on. When the storms of life come your way and you cannot find a resting place, that's when we need to know where to go and who to turn to so that we may survive the storms and tests; the only hope of surviving is in Christ Jesus. Christ Jesus is the only one who has the power to change our storms. For where Jesus is, there is peace and rest. Let's survive the test no matter what the devil brings our way, let's go to where Jesus is.

DAY 15: WHAT WAS JESUS' MISSION?

The Bible tells us in St. Luke 19:10: "For the son of man is come to seek and save that which is lost." Jesus was sent to be a redeemer of humanity that had lost their way to God the Father. So God sent his only begotten son to redeem man back to himself. Humanity was in a lost state wandering around without any direction; fallen from the first state that was created. God's son came to redeem, save and to bring the lost souls back to God, to condemn sin in the flesh. He also came to show humanity that God has a purpose and a divine plan for their lives. His job was to be the fulfillment of the law of God, but the law in itself was weak. Jesus came to instill this new law inside of every believer.

"For the law of the spirit of life in Christ Jesus hath made me free from the law of sin and death. For what the law could not, in that it was weak through the flesh, God sent his own Son in the likeness of sinful flesh, and for sin, condemned sin in the flesh." (Romans 8:2-3) Although the law was good; man could not live by it because they always found themselves in the midst of a struggle between doing right or wrong. Thanks be to God that his Son Jesus made a covering for the sins of all that believe in his Son Jesus name. Yes, we will have struggles, pains, heartaches, and problems, but no one is immune to these pains of life, nor are we insulated from suffering. Let me tell you; no one is allowed to slide through life without some problems. As we go through our struggles, we can see why Jesus died for us.

Galatians 3:13: "Christ hath redeemed us from the curse of the law, being made a curse for us: for it is written, Cursed is everyone that hangeth on a tree." Jesus had an assignment, a purpose, and he was chosen to do a service for his Father. Jesus' love for his father was so great that he wanted to give his life for the lives of the believers. Another reason Jesus came was to be an example of how a real Christian should live and how to love each other.

Jesus said: "I come not to do my will, but the will of my father which is in heaven."

I Peter 2:21: "For even hereunto were ye called: because Christ also suffered for us, leaving us an example, that ye should follow his steps."

Jesus serves as the perfect example of sacrifice for the greater good of the believers in Christ Jesus. We must strive to see the lesson in the mission that Jesus had and continue to work in the mission that God has given to us.

DAY 16: WHATEVER YOU DO, DO IT IN ITS SEASON!

Seasons are four different times of the year; spring, summer, fall, and winter, however; in some countries, there are only two seasons; the wet season, and the dry season. Seasons do not only relate to weather, but to the things that we go through in our daily lives. A lot of time people have trouble doing the things that they love to do because they are trying to do them out of season. There is a season for every purpose in life, and when we try to do them out of their season, they just don't work. Have you ever decided to go skiing in the summertime, or try to plant a garden, in the dead of winter? Do you know that everything has its own season, and its purpose, and that's the way that God made it be. Everything that exists in its season is for a reason and the glory of God and not man. When we look around, you can see the glory of God everywhere you look, because he is the creator and the heavenly father created everything to be in joy in its season. So there is a season of rain, of sunshine, of storms, and of calm. The Bible tells us in the book of Ecclesiastes 3:1; 17: "To everything, there is a season and a time to every purpose under heaven. I said in my heart; God shall judge the righteous and the wicked: for there is a time there for every purpose and every work." And when we have the foresight to walk, live, and exist in the season that God has placed us in to do his will, not only will God get the glory we will get his blessing. Every season brings some good days and some bad days, but how you handle the season will determine which direction you will go in your spiritual life.

God wants to bless everyone, but his blessing only comes in the season that God sends it, but if you are not ready to receive it or not in the right season, then you will miss your blessing. God wants to get the glory out of our lives. It is essential to know what season we are living in so that we can work in that period so that whatever you need to accomplish while we are in that season will be in God's will, and God will get the glory from everything you do.

DAY 17: YOUR DECISIONS WILL DETERMINE YOUR DESTINY

Deuteronomy 30:14-15: "But the word is very nigh unto thee, in thy mouth, and in thy heart, that thou mayest do it. See, I have set before thee this day life and good, and death and evil." The decisions that many people make often result in a lifetime of trouble, especially the decisions that are made in our youth. They don't take the time to think things out, and they do things on impulse lacking direction and purpose. These mistakes are often not realized until they are negatively manifested in different areas of their lives. For example; they think that they are in love at a young age and don't understand the responsibility of their actions. Nine months later they have a lifetime of responsibilities and troubles. The love that they thought they had then turns into resentment and can lead to hate because they were not truly ready for that kind of responsibility. As a result, those decisions will determine their destiny for the rest of their lives. Most do not take into consideration that they can no longer do the things that typical young people enjoy doing. Instead they must immediately take on the role of an adult. Which includes providing, protecting and nurturing a new life that has been given to them. With this type of responsibility, most young people are not mature enough to understand the consequences and results of their actions. We as people make bad decisions all the time and are unwilling to face the consequences of our actions commonly.

In many cases we are simply in denial. But the Bible says, "You will reap what you sow," so in other words, you plant the seed; it will grow, whether it's good or bad, it's coming up again in your life, and so often it comes up in the wrong season.

Proverbs 1:28-29: "Then shall they call upon me, but I will not answer; they shall seek me early, but they shall not find me. For that, they hated knowledge, and did not choose the fear of the Lord." In many cases we make choices, and we know that they are the wrong choices, but we do them any-way. For example; we don't have money to spend, so we get credit cards and max them out. When it's time to pay the bill we don't have the money, so we go and borrow more money to spend on bills, and then we find ourselves further in debt and don't know how we will pay them off. We are so consumed with fleshly desires that we only seek God for rescue instead of counsel and direction. We want him to get us out of the crisis that we got ourselves in, but how often do we consider the impact of our decisions on our destiny.

Proverbs 3:5-6 says: "Trust in the Lord with all your heart; and lean not unto thine own understanding. In all thy ways acknowledge him, and he shall direct thy paths." In conclusion, I encourage you to seek God in your decision making. With his divine guidance we can avoid a lot of the growing pains of life. Remember your decisions truly do determine your destiny.

DAY 18: DO YOU KNOW THAT GOD IS THE CREATOR AND NOT AN IMITATOR?

In the beginning, God created everything, and it was good. Even when he made humanity, he made him in his likeness and his image. He was a perfect being because he was in the image and likeness of God. But one-day mankind fell from the graces of God, because of sin. Mankind was listening to the imitator and not to the originator. So no longer was he a perfect being, but a falling one. That's why I often wonder why so many people would rather have an imitation opposed to having the real thing. Men have tried for thousands of years to prove that God does not exist. The more that they try to prove that he doesn't exist, they are actually showing that he does exist because he's in every part of creation. Men are trying to imitate what God has created while trying to change the way God has made us. One thing that man has not realized is that everything that God made and the way he made it was good. Genesis 1: 31 says: " And God saw everything that he had made and behold it was very good and the evening and the morning were the sixth day." There have been many imitators found throughout the bible in various settings. One of the early examples that comes to mind is the serpent in the garden of Eden. In the garden of Eden, the imitator lied to Adam and Eve.

He said to them, "If you eat this fruit you will be like God, knowing good from evil, and you won't die (death is the separation from God)." Knowing that God said not to eat of this fruit, for the day that you do, you will surely die. Adam and Eve were deceived into eating the fruit and were kicked out of the garden. In modern times these imitators can be seen as false prophets/teachers.

These are individuals who claim to be called by God but their teaching and beliefs do not align with God's word. They lead many astray and cause many to fall from the faith due to their personal agendas. God created man to live, and the imitator caused man to die. The Bible says that an imitator (the devil) comes to "steal, kill, and to destroy," but God comes to give us life and that more abundantly. So why be led by the imitator when you can be following the originator. Do you know that everything that God has made is good? The air that we breathe; the food that we eat and water that we drink; God created it all for our good, but men have taken it and are trying to recreate it. Now everything that we have that is good; men say that it is terrible for us. Where will it stop, God doesn't need our help, he created it all by himself, he doesn't need any little god or imitator, God just needs the people that he created to follow him and his word.

DAY 19: DO YOU KNOW THAT YOUR PURPOSE IS GREATER THAN YOUR PERSECUTION?

Purpose - "Is the reason for which something exists, done, or made; an intended, desired, result, aim, or goal."

Persecute - "To be subject to harassing or cruel treatment, as because of race, religion or beliefs."

Isaiah 14:27 says, "For the Lord of hosts hath purposed, and who shall disannul it? And his hand is stretched out, and who shall turn it back?" No matter what you say, what you believe, and even what you do without the divine purpose of God in you, your life is always lacking something to define it. In other words, you will find yourself bankrupt and without a purpose. So many people are confused or don't know what their purpose is here on earth. They tend to wander aimlessly never accomplishing anything but constantly searching for something. There are some who are in search of family, while some are seeking value from others, among those who are searching simply for love. There are so many people who have unanswered questions about who they are and where they come from. Maybe you have found yourself wondering and questioning yourself about the same things. One thing to remember is you did not come into this world by accident or chance. Even if your parents weren't ready, God had already purpose it to be, and because of that purpose you have great value and worth that you might not know, nor people cannot see, but God can, and he knows what his plan and purpose is for your life.

In the book of Acts 26:16, the author writes, "But rise, and stand upon thy feet: for I have appeared unto thee for this purpose, to make thee a minister and a witness both of these things which thou hast seen, and of those things in which I will appear unto thee."

Sometimes we have to suffer for no apparent reason, but it has a purpose and God knows our purpose. If we seek him; he will show us what the reasons are. Jeremiah 1:4-5: "Then the word of the Lord came unto me, saying. Before I formed thee in the belly I knew thee; and before thou comest forth out of the womb, I sanctified thee, and I ordained thee a prophet unto the nations." By focusing on ourselves, God will never reveal to us our purpose in life. God created man, and he established his plan in man. God gave his plan and purpose to man, but the evil one deceived them, and it was lost.

The Bible says you must, "seek it and you will find it." God's purpose took into account human error. He never does anything wrong or accidentally; he never makes mistakes, he always has a reason for everything he does and creates. He will give us the meaning of the purpose of our life if we ask him. We can only discover our life purpose if we seek it, and make God the reference point of our life.

Paraphrasing Romans 12:1-8, the scripture is saying the only way to understand our purpose and ourselves is by having a relationship with God, and to acknowledge who he is, what he has done and what he is doing in our lives daily. That's why your purpose is always greater than your persecution. You will still have troubles, problems, and many hills to climb, but God will never put more on you than you can bear. So let's find out what our purpose in life is so that we can please God. And always trust God's timing.

DAY 20: WHAT TIME DO YOU HAVE? DO YOU HAVE THE TIME TO WAIT ON GOD?

So many People pray for God to do something in their lives, but won't take the time to wait for him to answer their prayers. They act as if God owes them something but do you know that God breathed into the nostrils of man, and he became a living soul. So besides his son, Jesus, the breath of life was the most personal and magnificent gift God could give to man. So we should take the time to wait for him when we ask him for something; because God wants his people to have the very best of everything and as the saying goes there's a time and a season for everything. If we rush God to answer our prayers and the season isn't right then, you may get an answer, but it might not be the one you're expecting. So ask yourself the question: do you have the time to wait on God?

The old saying is, "He may not come when you want him but he's always on time." In other words, he's an on time God. There is a story of a man named Job, he was a man that was righteous in the eyes of God. The devil came before God to falsely accuse him, to obtain leverage so that he could tempt him to do wrong, no matter what the devil did to Job, he still waited and trusted in God.

Job said, "The Lord giveth and the Lord taketh away, bless' it be the name of the Lord." Job knew where his help came from, and we should know where our help comes from too. Job also said, "Though he slays me, yet will I trust in him: but I will maintain my own ways before him. He also shall be my salvation: for a hypocrite shall not come before him. (Job 12: 15-16) Job had the time to wait on God no matter how long it took. He was going to wait because he knew that God was going to restore back to him all that the devil had stolen from him.

So do you have the time to wait for the Lord like Job? We think that our lives are so busy that we don't take the time to wait for other people to help us before we try to do things ourselves. When it's all over and done, we find that things didn't go right and end up hurting ourselves more because we couldn't wait for the help that we needed from someone else. The book of Ecclesiastes 3:1 says, "To everything, there is a season, and a time to every purpose under the heavens." We always want things done when we want it done, but the timing might not be the right time to do what we want to do. If we learn to wait we will find that everything will work itself out evenly. God has a time for everything, and he will work it out for you at his timing and not yours. You can get impatient if you want to, but you can't hurry God. He always knows what is best for you and he will come when the timing is right.

DAY 21: DO YOU KNOW THAT THE CYCLE HAS TO STOP SOMEWHERE?

Somebody may ask the question what cycle are you talking about, and that is the cycle of breaking generational curses within the family tree. A generational curse is simply repeating the same old cycle over again. So many times people don't realize that the things they do may not only affect them but the generations to come. These habits and bad choices will continue from one generation to the next generation. Numbers 14:18 says, "The Lord is long-suffering, and of great mercy, forgiving iniquity and transgression, and by no means clearing the guilty, visiting the iniquity of the fathers upon the children unto the third and fourth generation." You will find so many young women having children at young ages when they are still children themselves. When their children grow up to be about the same age, then they start having children too, and repeating the same old cycle that their mothers repeated. This cycle seems to go on and on and on until somebody decides to stop and break this cycle. It will take many prayers to break this kind of generational curse once it has started. There are so many types of examples that we can talk about, but there is only one answer, and that is "prayer." The Bible tells us that "prayer changes things" and if we want to break the generational curses in our lives rather than be drug abusers, alcoholics, prostitutes, physical abusers, mental abusers, emotional abusers, sexual abusers, liars, cheater, thieves and so on. We need to recognize the cycle; fall on our knees and start praying that God will break those cycles that are in our family lines.

We all have generational curses rather than whether we realize it or not. It is up to us to make the decision to continue that curse or break those strongholds over our lives. Those types of cycles have to stop and why not start with you? The Bible tells us in the book of James 5: 15: "And the prayer of faith shall save the sick, and the Lord shall raise him up; and if he has sinned, they shall be forgiven him." When we realize that we have these generational curses in our lives; don't give up, and let them continue to control you. Let's break the cycle and begin to pray because prayer is the only answer to breaking a generation curse. Prayer is the answer and faith in God will see you through. No matter how bad it may seem, when you pray and have faith in God, he will listen to what you have to say.

DAY 22: DO YOU KNOW THAT THERE IS HOPE FOR A BRIGHTER DAY!

As a believer, our hope is supposed to be in Christ Jesus. In whom do you place your hope? Are you putting your hopes in the right one or the right thing? As we look around in our world today, we see that people don't have their hope in Christ Jesus. They seem to have their faith in everything that is in this world. The love of money, sex, and fame; No matter what they have to do to get there, they will do it. What the bible says is wrong, while what the world says is right. We look and see that the world is in bad shape, there are wars all over the world, and people are killing each other for no reason. There is no peace to be found yet the world says everything is alright because their hope is in the world and not in Christ Jesus.

Hope - "To have confidence in or expectancy of."

The Bible tells us that hope stands for both the act of hope and the things hoped for. Our hope does not always arise from personal desires or wishes but from God; who himself is the believer's hope. "Blessed be the father of our Lord Jesus Christ, which according to his abundant mercy hath begotten us again unto a lively hope by the resurrection of Jesus Christ from the dead. To an inheritance incorruptible, and undefiled, and that fadeth not away, reserved in heaven for you." (I Peter 1: 3-4) When we think about a genuine hope; it is neither in one wishful thinking, nor is it in one idle thought, but can be found in a firm assurance that things that are not seen are coming shortly because of our faith and hope in Christ Jesus.

"For we are saved by hope: but hope that is seen is not hope: for what a man seeth, why doth he yet hope for? But if we hope that we see it, then do we wait for it?" (Romans 8: 24- 25) Genuine hope also will distinguish the believers from the unbelievers. Those who have no hope or their hope is in the wrong things and those whose hope is in Christ Jesus. If your hope is in something else, then you have no one to depend on because man, material things, and this world will let you down.

True Christians know that hope comes from knowing who God is and having a relationship with him and his son Jesus Christ. "Now the God of hope fills you with all joy and peace in believing, that ye may abound in hope, through the power of the Holy Ghost." (Romans 15:13)

DAY 23: THERE'S GOT TO BE SOMETHING REAL ABOUT YOU!

There is a story I heard a long time ago about a little boy and a little old lady. *One day the little boy wanted to go play with his friends at their favorite water hole, and his mother told him he had to be careful because he had to go down to the river to get there. Certain parts of the river were rough with heavy currents, so the little boy told his mother that he would be careful. As he began to walk towards the river, he heard a soft voice saying, "Please...Please...save me." The little boy ran to the bank of the river, and in the distance, he saw a little old lady being carried by the current down the river. As the little old lady passed by him, the little boy stepped out into the river and reached out to try to grab her by the hair as she passed by him, but when he looked in his hands, all he saw was the wig that the woman was wearing. When he realized that he didn't save the woman he thought if I could just get in front of her down by the bend in the river where the water slows down then I should be able to grab her. So he ran as fast as he could to get ahead of her. When he got to the bend in the river, he got in the water as he heard the little old woman coming near yelling out, "Please... Please...someone save me." As he saw her coming, he reached out to grab her by her hand and pulled with all his might. When he looked at her, he realized that all he had was her artificial arm. He jumped out of the water and ran to the next spot where he thought that he could save the little old woman. He jumped in the boat and paddle as hard as he could to the center of the river and waited for the little old lady to pass by.*

When he saw her coming he reached out to grab hold of her, he grabbed her by the leg but once again he only had her artificial leg in his hand. And the little old lady continued to float up and down in the river crying, "O Please...please... someone save me."

The little boy cried out with a loud voice, "Little old lady, I try to, but there's got to be something real about you."

Looking back upon that story it is easy to find humor in it, but have we taken the time to focus on the true meaning of the story? When I say, "There's got to be something real about you," I am saying that you should not have a false profession of your faith, of who you are and what you stand on. So many people don't live the way that they profess. There is no substance to the lives that they live and what they portray to others. Like the little old lady, they present a false identity so that people won't know who or what they truly are.

When you profess that you are a Christian, all your choices and decisions are magnified to the unbelievers. The enemy uses this tactic to try to discredit your walk with Christ and put more pressure on you to stumble in the eyes of the unbelievers. There is a popular saying that states: "Your life may be the only bible that the unbeliever may ever read." This is very true and plays a significant role in many unbelievers' decision to consider the Christian walk or stay away from it. If your life is not right as a Christian, an unbeliever may choose not to follow God, resulting in another lost soul.

The Bible tells us, "Not everyone that saith unto me, Lord, Lord, shall enter into the kingdom of heaven; but he that doeth the will of my father which is in heaven." (Matthew 7: 21) This scripture is simply saying that talking a good game is not enough to get into heaven. We must have a genuine relationship with Christ and this must be represented in the way we live our lives.

So if you are not sincere about your profession of faith, you will not make it into the kingdom of heaven, and could cost someone else the opportunity also. So, "There's got to be something real about you."

DAY 24: PLEASE DON'T JUMP THE GUN!

When God makes a promise, it's always made with a specification, which is the fact that we have to wait on him. This is because he knows what's best for us and he knows when we need it. So don't jump the gun!

Sometimes it's easier to try to help God, but God doesn't need our help. He just needs us to be obedient to him and wait on him. He may not come when we want him, but he's always right on time. When we get in a hurry, we make mistakes, but when we wait patiently on the Lord, good things can happen in our lives. For example, there are some of us that desire a new car or house. We rush and push and end up having to settle for less than what we originally wanted. Hence, jumping the gun. We just can't wait until the time is right or until God says it's right. We want it right now, and we want it the way we want it and not when the time is right, or when God says so. The Bible teaches us in the book of Isaiah 40: 31: "But they that wait upon the Lord shall renew their strength; they shall mount up with wings as eagles; they shall run, and not be weary, and they shall walk, and not faint." Waiting sometimes is the hardest thing to do for most people, but as Christian, we know that God always comes when the time is right. He always knows when the people of God are ready to receive his promises. If we learn how to wait on God, he promises us our strength renewed, to exalt us, to give to us spiritual progress, and spiritual power. The bottom line is that God wants us to trust him for everything and in every way in all things. When we jump the gun it lets him know that we don't fully trust him. When we can't fully trust him, then he can't work on our behalf.

When God makes a promise, it's always made with a specification, which is the fact that we have to wait on him. This is because he knows what's best for us and he knows when we need it. So don't jump the gun!

Sometimes it's easier to try to help God, but God doesn't need our help. He just needs us to be obedient to him and wait on him. He may not come when we want him, but he's always right on time. When we get in a hurry, we make mistakes, but when we wait patiently on the Lord, good things can happen in our lives. For example, there are some of us that desire a new car or house. We rush and push and end up having to settle for less than what we originally wanted. Hence, jumping the gun. We just can't wait until the time is right or until God says it's right. We want it right now, and we want it the way we want it and not when the time is right, or when God says so. The Bible teaches us in the book of Isaiah 40: 31: "But they that wait upon the Lord shall renew their strength; they shall mount up with wings as eagles; they shall run, and not be weary, and they shall walk, and not faint." Waiting sometimes is the hardest thing to do for most people, but as Christian, we know that God always comes when the time is right. He always knows when the people of God are ready to receive his promises. If we learn how to wait on God, he promises us our strength renewed, to exalt us, to give to us spiritual progress, and spiritual power. The bottom line is that God wants us to trust him for everything and in every way in all things. When we jump the gun it lets him know that we don't fully trust him. When we can't fully trust him, then he can't work on our behalf. If we don't have the faith that we need for God to work for us, then we will continue in the cycle of making hasty decisions that lead us where we don't want to be.

In the Christian walk, Faith is the most important thing that we can have and without faith, we cannot please God. Hebrews 11:6: "But without faith, it is impossible to please him:

for him that cometh to God must believe that he is and that he is a rewarder of them that diligently seek him." Faith is the key to open up the promises of God. When we look at some of the heroes of faith in the bible, we can see that without their faith, God could not work on their behalf. Noah prepared an ark to save him and his whole family. He couldn't see it but he believed and through faith they all were saved. Abraham was called out by God and was obedient to the voice of God and found favor with him. He followed God's commands by faith and his seed was blessed because of his faithfulness. These are just a few of the many examples that the bible shows us of genuine people of faith and how faith will move God. When God speaks of faith, it is the substance of things hoped for and evidence of things not seen. Meaning you can't see it; you can't feel it; you just have to wait on God as a believer to receive it. The biggest message overall is to wait on God because his timing is always perfect!

DAY 25: BEING CONFORMED TO THE IMAGE OF HIS SON!

Today's topic is focused on being conformed to the image of Gods' son Jesus Christ. Let's first look at what it means to be confirm. It is to be or become similar in form, nature, or character. An image is defined as a physical likeness or representation of a person, animal or thing. In order to be conformed we must first go through a process or processing. This process is a series of actions directed to conform us to his likeness. The first step of this series starts with the confession of our sins.

"That if thou shalt confess with thy mouth the Lord Jesus and shalt believe in thine heart that God hath raised him from the dead, thou shalt be saved." (Romans 10:9) This two part process is broken down into confession and believing in one's heart. The confession is when a person realizes that they need God and their lives are not going anywhere without him. After this realization they come to God to repent of their sins. Following repentance the next step is believing in one's heart. This is when the person turns from their evil ways and begins to trust, love, and follow the ways of Jesus Christ. With these changes comes a newness of life. When the image of God's son is in a person's life; they have the attributes and qualities of him in them. When the image of his son is in a person's life, its reflection is like looking in a mirror and seeing God's son. You will begin to walk like him, talk like him and reflect his teachings in everything that you do. We also must have a personal relationship with him daily.

Having a personal relationship continues the fellowship of God. "For whom he did foreknow, he also did predestinate to be conformed to the image of his Son, that he might be the firstborn among many brethren." (Romans 8:29) God knew before we were born that we were foreordained to be in the likeness of his son Jesus Christ. To be created in the image of the son of God means we the people of God have the ability, the God giving right and privilege of knowing who God is.

The right to serve him, love him and to see that we can fulfill our God-given purpose and potential in this life. Romans 12:2: "Do not be conformed to this world, but be transformed by the renewing of your mind, that you may prove what is the good, pleasing, and perfect will of God."

DAY 26: WHAT STATE OF MIND WERE YOU IN BEFORE YOU MET CHRIST?

Everyone who does not know the Lord is condemned. The Bible says, "There is therefore now no condemnation to them which are in Christ Jesus, who walk not after the flesh, But after the spirit." (Romans 8:1) The word condemns, or condemnation has the same meaning: to declare a person guilty and worthy of their punishment. The Bible tells us that at birth we were condemned because of sin. When Adam sinned in the Garden of Eden, all flesh from that day forward were born into sin. So, we have a sinful nature and everything that we do is of a sinful nature. Paul said in the book of Romans that we struggle and war against sin in our flesh, and he used the term flesh as being carnal minded. And a carnally minded person cannot please God because a carnal minded man is an enemy of God. What state of mind were you in before you met Christ? The only one that can answer this question is you and God. In today's world, people's minds are on everything but God and his word. If your mind is not focused on Jesus, then the answer to the question is that your mind was in a carnal state.

The Apostle Paul instructed us where to keep our minds when he said, "Let this mind be in you, which was also in Christ Jesus." (Philippians 2:5) Before we met Christ, our mind was all over the place. Thanks be to God that he sent his son Jesus Christ to be a sacrifice for the sins of all. To show us that we can have the mind that God intended for us to have from the beginning. Jesus made the statement that, "He did not come to condemn the world, but through him, man might be saved."

His mission was to come and show men how to live a truly Christian life and to be an example of whom and what Christ is in the life of all believers. To die upon the cross to bear the sin that belonged to people of God. "For God so loved the world that he gave his only begotten son, that whosoever believeth in him should not perish, but have everlasting life. For God sent not his son into the world to condemn the world: but that the world through him might be saved. He that believeth on him is not condemned: but he that believeth not is condemned already because he hath not believed in the name of the only begotten son of God." (St. John 3:16-18.)

Since we have experienced God's gracious pardon from our sin, we ought to practice forgiveness, to love one another, avoid condemning others and pointing the finger of blame. For this is having the mind of Christ. "Condemn not, and you shall not be condemned." (Luke 6:37)

DAY 27: PRIDE

The Bible teaches us that pride comes before the fall. In a book by Ben Carson: A Thought on Pride it talks about when some people begin to experience a degree of success; they become overly confident in their abilities. These swollen-headed types of people usually cease from learning. They tend to feel as if they know everything already. They tend to do very little and always think about themselves. For example, instead of singing the hymn: "How Great thou Art," their words sound like: "How Great I Am." Many people fall into this category without realizing that they are full of pride, conceited, self-centered, egotistic, and vain; having a high opinion of oneself. They think that the world revolves around them and they also think more of themselves than of other people. They have an unfavorable idea or high opinion of their self-worth, with a negative emotion toward anybody other than themselves.

God said that he hates the spirit of pride. "The fear of the Lord is to hate evil: pride, and arrogance, and the evil way, and the froward mouth, do I hate." (Proverbs 8:13) One of the things that God commanded his people to do is to resist worldliness. Worldliness is the lust of the flesh (the passion for sensual satisfaction), the lust of the eyes (the inordinate desire for the finer things in life), and the pride of life (self-satisfaction in who they are, what they have, and what they have done). Some people are so prideful and selfish that they want to be and live like people that are well off or rich. Their pride will not let them see that everybody doesn't get the opportunity to live that way.

In the book of 1 John 2: 15-17: "Love not the world, neither the things that are in the world: if any man loves the world, the love of the Father is not in him. For all that is in the world, the lust of the flesh, and the lust of the eyes, and the pride of life, is not of the Father but is of the world. And they would passeth away, and the lust thereof: but he that doeth the will of God abideth forever." Here is an example of a man with pride in the Bible. The book of Daniel 4: 30-33, talks about a king by the name of Neb-u-chad-nezzar.

The king says, "Is not this great Babylon that I have built for the house of the kingdom by the might of my power, and for the honor of my majesty?" People with pride always want other people to know what they have done, and how well they have done it. Everything that you will accomplish in your life is nothing compared to their accomplishment. The king built Babylon and gave himself all the credit, boasting about what he had done.

Verse 31: "While the word was still in his mouth, there was a voice from heaven saying, O King Nebuchadnezzar, to thee it is spoken; the kingdom is departed from thee. And they shall drive thee from men, and thy dwelling shall be with the beasts of the fields: they shall make thee eat grass and oxen and seven times shall pass over thee, until thou know that the highest ruleth in the kingdom of men, and giveth it to whomsoever he will." So it doesn't pay to think more highly or boast about what you have done, but to be thankful for what God has done and what he will do in your life.

This reiterates the previous statement: "Pride comes before the fall." Therefore I challenge you to be humble, seek God and always remember it is he that has equipped us with what it takes to be successful.

DAY 28: DO YOU KNOW WE ALL HAVE OUR SHARE OF UPS AND DOWNS?

No matter who you are or what you have done in your life, you will still have troubles, but the best is yet to come. Even though we see the economy down; major corporations are falling apart, fighting and wars all over the world, food and the livestock market are in a downward spin and the money that seems to be invincible at one time may run out. Still, the best is yet to come. Sometimes when we look at other people's lives it's easy to think that we are the only ones' having troubles. It's often hard to look past our own problems to see that everyone has them, it just looks different. Ask yourself this question: Will I be able to handle it or will it handle me? How your troubles affect you depends on how you handle your problems. Everyone is going through trials and tribulations and no one gets the chance to bypass this. How you face your challenges and troubles determines your outcome. Do you know where your help comes from? The Bible tells us, "These things I have spoken unto you, that in me ye might have peace. In the world ye shall have tribulation (trouble): but be of good cheer; I have overcome the world." (St. John 16: 33)

Songwriter Norman Hutchins wrote: "It makes no difference what you're going through, you can make it, God will see you though." It may seem like you're up one day and down the next, but just hold your head up and don't look back and you can go through all of your challenging days.

Yes, you too can overcome the obstacles that the enemy tries to put in your life by turning them over to the Lord; he is the one that can fix it all for you. King David was one that knew how to overcome the troubles in his life. He knew that when he got into trouble to call on God through prayer with a professing heart and God would hear him and help him to overcome all of his problems. He knew that when he was down God would pick him up, turn him around and put his feet back on the right path. All he had to do was just trust and believe in the Lord and his word. We too need to know how to get up like David and not let our problems keep us down. We can use our experiences as testimony that God will see you though. Proclaiming if he can do it for me then he can do it for you! We must remember that as believers we are not exempt from troubles but we are equipped with the tools to overcome them.

DAY 29: DO YOU KNOW TO BE LOVED, YOU MUST FIRST LOVE YOURSELF!

Love is one of the most essential words in the human language. It is the most significant word in the Bible. You may ask why it is the greatest word in the Bible and that is because God said that he is "Love." So if God is God and God is Love who is greater than him. Most people mistake love for lust. Lust is an emotion or feeling of intense desire in one's body. Lust can take many forms such as; the lust for money, lust for knowledge, the lust for sex, and the lust of power. Lust will make some people do some strange and unusual things. Due to lust, some people will find themselves in bad and toxic relationships. Although the relationship has run its course, they find that every time they start a new relationship they seem to attract the same type of person that they had before. Another example is those that weren't fortunate enough to have parents who showed them love when they were children. For many as adults they search for this type of love in romantic relationships. This can sometimes be seen in relationships where there is a significant age gap between the partners and they have more of a parent/child dynamic opposed to a husband/wife dynamic. Another example is individuals that suffered abuse as a child who didn't get the help that they needed when they were young. They were left to grow up thinking that the only way that they will find love is to let someone else abuse them. Without proper support these children could ultimately become adults who accept physical, emotional and psychological abuse mistaking this for true love.

These examples reinforce the fact that some people truly don't understand that before they can be loved, they have to love themselves first. The Bible teaches us that "God is love" so to find true love one must first find God and give him all of our problems. He is the only one that can change our situations. So when we find God, we find true love and when we find true love, we can then find ourselves. "For God, who is rich in mercy, for his great love wherewith he loved us." (Ephesians 2:4) God's love goes beyond what man can think, feel, see, believe, hope in, and hope for because God loves us even when we don't love ourselves. He looks beyond our faults, and he sees what the needs are in our lives.

"Behold what manner of love the Father hath bestowed upon us, that we should be called the sons of God: wherefore the world knoweth us not because it knows him not. Beloved now are we the sons of God, and it doth not yet appear what we shall be: but we know that, when he shall appear, we shall be like him; for we shall see him as he is." (I John 3: 1-2) Therefore because God loves us so much and we have him in our lives, then we can begin to love ourselves and our fellow man.

DAY 30: DO YOU KNOW THAT GOD HAS IT ALREADY WORKED OUT?

It may be hard to believe but in every temptation, every sin, every problem that may come up in your life, God has already worked it out for you. These situations function in our lives to build towards God's will for our lives. These trials and tribulation may be used by God to make us more mature and stronger than before. It is an opportunity for us to show God that we have grown and developed into a mature Christian. Ask yourself, "Is God working everything out in my life? If not, why?"

Take a moment to reflect on situations that you have experienced in the past. Can you recall a time where you were encompassed in trying to figure out a solution to the issue just to discover that God had already worked it out for you? It is second nature for many of us to focus on reaching a solution that fits what we think is best while ignoring what God's plan is for us truly. This is the point where our faith is truly tested. All you have to do is to have a little faith, and let God work on your favor. When Temptations come into your life, look at them as stepping stones instead of stumbling blocks. You can use them to grow in Christ Jesus and to develop into what Christ wants you to be. When we realize that temptations are just as much an opportunity to do what is right then to do what is wrong, that shows that we have grown and matured in Christ Jesus.

"Blessed is the man that endureth temptation: for when he is tried, he shall receive the crown of life, which the Lord hath promised. Let no man say when he is tempted; I am tempted of God: for God cannot be tempted with evil, neither tempted he any man. But every man is tempted, when he is drawn away by his lust, and enticed." (James 1: 12-14) Temptations will simply provide a choice to do what is right or what is wrong.

The Bible says, "Choose this day whom ye will save," which simply means that the choice is yours. While temptation is one of the weapons that

Satan uses on believers to destroy us, God is willing to use it to develop us spiritually. Christ directs the people of God to resist temptation, and if you resist temptation, God promises to bless them that do so. He also directs us to pray for deliverance from being exposed to or surrendering to it.

"And lead us not into temptation, but deliver us from evil: for thine is the kingdom, and the power, and glory, for every: A-man." God will not allow his people to encounter temptation too hard for them to resist but always will make a way for them to deal with it, and to prove their faithfulness to him.

To My Husband

We have been through so many journeys during our time as husband and wife that God has kept us through. I have on so many occasions watched you fight the good fight of faith and God came through every time. I am so proud of what you have been able to accomplish with God as your lead and guide and the ambition you have that has driven you. You are truly a man after God's own heart and a great husband, father, and grandfather. It is an honor to stand beside you as you stand for Christ, and we will continue to minister to the lost for whom he has sent us. Keep up the awesome work, I know your parents are proud because I know I am.

With all my love – *Liz*

IN LOVING MEMORY

I just wanted to take a moment to recognize my parents and to say thank you for all that you have poured into me. I would not be who I am today if it weren't for who you raised me to be. You both were great examples of what a Christian should be and I thank you both for that. Every day I wish I had more time with you, but one thing I do know is if I continue to follow Christ, I will see you again. Continue to watch over me.

Love, Ray

One day I noticed that I had been writing down things that I had been thinking about and I was talking to my wife and daughter about some of the things that interest me from my studies. They saw how excited I got when talking about the many topics that came to mind, then my daughters asked "why not write a book?" I began to pray and ask the lord for his guidance, and then I started to record all of my thoughts and conversations I had with other people. I developed my topics from sermons that I heard from other ministers, sermons that I've shared with the congregation that I lead, and thoughts from songs that I have listened to. Through my studying of god's word I understand that people are looking for the secret of life and most of the time it's right there in front of them. Their eyes might be blinded to the truth and god's word is our guideline to understanding what the secret of life is. Proverbs 4:7b says, "And with all thy getting, get an understanding." Getting an understanding is the key to opening up new opportunities. Understanding also enables one to see better ways of dealing with their problems, and mending their broken relationship with others and even understanding themselves. Although you may not agree with some of my thoughts, topics, and ideas; I encourage you to pray about it and just remember god's word doesn't lie.

"Ask, and it shall be given you: seek, and ye shall find; knock and it shall be opened unto you." (Matthew 7:7) God will better open up your understanding of his word if you are willing to seek him.

"If any of you lack wisdom, let him ask of god that giveth to all men liberally, and upbraideth not: and it shall be given him." (James 1:5) It is my hope that this book will assist you in hearing what god's word is saying to you. Just remember they are my thoughts and you do not have to agree with my views. I am giving them to you the way that god has dealt with me. All of my thoughts and comments come from the holy bible, so I hope that you enjoy it, God bless you.

Dr. Willie R hill Sr., Ph.D.

Photograph by Bigshot Photo

www.ingramcontent.com/pod-product-compliance
Lightning Source LLC
Chambersburg PA
CBHW061355140726
47997CB00003B/1213